The Littlest Lion

THE LION CUBS OF OMAHA'S HENRY DOORLY ZOO & AQUARIUM

STORY BY CAROL BICAK • PHOTOS BY CHRIS MACHIAN AND KENT SIEVERS OF THE OMAHA WORLD-HERALD

No one expected five of us. But on a really cold December night
our mom, Mfisha, an African lion at Omaha's Henry Doorly Zoo,
gave birth to three girls and two boys. We were her first babies,
and she was surprised to have five at one time, because lions
usually have two or three cubs in a litter.

My name is Zuri. At a little over 2 pounds, I was much weaker
than my sisters and brothers. I couldn't get any food.
The vets thought I would die so they took me to the zoo hospital.

They put me in a warm, lighted box
because I didn't have the other cubs to snuggle with.
And they gave me special food.

All these strangers — I was pretty sure
they weren't lions — scared me.
But after a few days I began to feel better and get stronger.

In a week, the doctors took me back to my family.
I was happy to go back to Mom and the others,
but the zookeepers were worried.
Would my family accept me?

Not at first. My brothers and sisters seemed glad
to have one more playmate. But Mom thought
I smelled like humans and didn't seem to want me.
In fact, she kind of lost interest in all five of us.

Luckily, Aunt Ahadi, Mom's sister who lives with us,
jumped in and fed us. She must have talked to Mom,
because Mom came back and even licked me.
Guess she thought I smelled OK.
We think she's the best mom ever, but we love Auntie too.

I still had to eat special food for a while, but one day
I decided Mom's milk was enough. That was that.

By the time our one-month birthday rolled around, we were a big,
happy family. We got a meat cake to celebrate being a month old,
but Mom and Aunt Ahadi enjoyed it more than we did.

Two months later, the zoo had a naming contest for us.
Visitors turned in more than 5,000 names, so the zoo had a hard time
choosing. Finally they told us the winning names — all African.
My name, Zuri, means beautiful flower. My brothers are Taj and Josiri,
and my sisters are Kya and Leela. We love our names.

All five of us have trainers. We saw them work with Mom and Auntie,
and it looked like fun. Although our trainers often call us clowns,
they don't teach us to do tricks like circus animals.

We learn things that help our keepers, like coming when called.
Hardest to learn is standing still. We want to wiggle and be silly.
Our training feels like playing most of the time.
Plus we get treats as we learn.

When it comes to trying something new, we always wait
for Mom to say it's OK. Like the first time we got to go outside
after winter was over. Mom went into our outdoor home and
checked every corner to make sure it was safe. Then we followed.
Everyone was a little nervous, but I took a deep breath and led the way.
Now we have so much fun outside.

Mom always tries out new toys, like straw bales
or balls or stuffed animals, and she tastes new food first.
She shows us how to climb on the rocks or tree limbs.
If she says something is safe, then we can try it.
We still fall down a lot when it comes to big jumps and climbing.

One of the most fun things we do is explore.
I may be small, but I'm braver than my brothers and sisters.
They are afraid of new things, even after Mom says it's OK.
So I usually try those things first.
My brothers and sisters can be shy around people too.

When they see how brave I am and how much fun I have,
they follow my lead. It makes me proud.

The trainers call me mischievous, because I
sometimes get into trouble and lead the others into trouble.

You'd think Taj, biggest of us all, would be the leader.

But he just likes to stay close to Mom.

I think it's because he likes to eat so much.

The five of us stick together. We're usually either all inside or all outside.
We like to play games like follow the leader and tag. We pounce
on our toys, wrestle each other and climb all over Mom and Auntie.
Sometimes we bite their tails, which makes them a little mad at us.

Once we saw a ball floating in the pool in our outdoor space
and tried to reach it. We couldn't and fell into the water.
Lions aren't supposed to like water, but we had fun that day.

You might be surprised that baby lions have spots.
When we get older they will disappear and we will be tan colored.
For now, the dark spots come in handy because they help our trainers
tell us apart. When boy lions grow up, they have bushy manes
on their heads. Josiri and Taj won't look like that for a few years.
But if you look carefully, you can see they have sideburns.

We love to take naps. We eat. Then we sleep. We play.

Then we sleep. In fact, we sleep 20 hours a day.

When we reached 6 months old, we had grown a lot.

Big Taj weighed in at 78 pounds. I told you he likes to eat!

I weighed only 43 pounds, still the runt,

but I am healthy and strong.

Size isn't always the most important thing.

Mom has told us we all will have to be really brave in the future,
because we can't stay with her at the Omaha zoo forever.
We will be going to new zoos to start our own families.

Just like children grow up and leave their parents' homes, so will we.
I can't wait for another adventure!

The life of a lion

Lions once roamed most of Africa as well as parts of Europe, the Middle East and Asia. As recently as the 1940s, about 450,000 lions were in the wild. Today that number has shriveled to fewer than 21,000, mostly in sub-Saharan Africa. The species could be threatened with extinction unless steps are taken to stop trophy hunting, reduce the use of poisonous pesticides on crops and halt destruction of lion habitat.

Lions are the most social of the big cats. They live in family groups called prides, which can include a few males, several females and cubs. Lionesses nurse each other's young. Pride members have been observed being affectionate, grooming each other, purring and head rubbing.

The male lion defends the pride's territory, sometimes as much as 100 square miles. Female lions are the hunters, and they often hunt as teams. Zebras, wildebeest, impala, giraffes and wild hogs make up their main prey. Lions hunt mostly at night and sleep up to 20 hours a day. They can eat up to 40 pounds of meat a day. Their roar is possible because of a special larynx. That roar can be heard up to five miles away.

Because the breeding history of the Omaha zoo's five cubs is known, they are valuable to the Association of Zoos and Aquariums Species Survival Plan. They can be matched with lions in other zoos to keep the gene pool of captive lions healthy. Zoos also are making changes in the way lions are exhibited, trying to give them space and more natural surroundings.

Facts

Scientific name: Panthera leo krugeri (South African)

Life span: 12-15 years in the wild, longer in captivity

Litter size: Usually 2-3

Gestation: 110 days

Average height: 42-52 inches

Average length: 6 or 7 feet

Average weight: 400 lbs. for males, 280 lbs. for females

Top speed: 50 mph

Mfisha

Cubs' mother
Born: July 6, 2007
Weight: 305 lbs.
Came from: Tautphaus Park
    Zoo in Idaho Falls, Idaho

Ahadi

Cubs' aunt, Mfisha's sister
Born: Jan. 4, 2008
Weight: 281 lbs.
Came from: Tautphaus Park
    Zoo in Idaho Falls, Idaho

Mr. Big

Cubs' father
Born: Aug. 15, 1999
Weight: 500 lbs.
Came from: Oklahoma City Zoo

Zuri

Name means: Beautiful flower
Birth weight: 2.06 lbs.
Six-month weight: 43 lbs.
Personality: Fearless, playful

Taj

Name means: Crown
Birth weight: 3.25 lbs.
Six-month weight: 78 lbs.
Personality: Calm, loves to eat

Leela

Name means: Night beauty
Birth weight: 2.95 lbs.
Six-month weight: 50 lbs.
Personality: Stubborn, loves toys

Kya

Name means: Diamond in the sky
Birth weight: 3.5 lbs.
Six-month weight: 60 lbs.
Personality: Sassy, loves food

Josiri

Name means: Brave
Birth weight: 3.3 lbs.
Six-month weight: 55 lbs.
Personality: Moody, shy

The cubs' story

Mfisha's five cubs arrived at Omaha's Henry Doorly Zoo & Aquarium on Dec. 29, 2012. They were the first lion cubs born at the Omaha zoo since 1994.

Dr. Doug Armstrong and his staff worked hard to save Zuri, the runt. Separating Zuri from the rest of the litter was a huge gamble. Animal experts said returning her to the family couldn't be done, that Mfisha never would accept the little lion.

Mfisha did temporarily lose interest in being a mother when Zuri was re-introduced. Then Aunt Ahadi stepped in. Ahadi, Mfisha's sister, took over nursing duties, something not unusual in the wild. Eventually Mfisha resumed her role as mother. Unfortunately, Ahadi, who also was pregnant, lost her cubs. But even when her nieces and nephews were six months old, she still was as involved in raising them as Mfisha, who has turned out to be a wonderful mother.

You may wonder about their dad, Mr. Big. Since the cubs' birth, he has lived in another area of the Omaha zoo's Cat Complex with a lioness named Nala. She doesn't like Mfisha, Ahadi or the cubs. She and Mr. Big were paired for years before Mfisha or Ahadi were born. At one point it was thought Mr. Big would join his family of cubs, but it was decided Nala needed him more. Because lions are social animals, Nala probably wouldn't survive if left alone.

Omaha's Henry Doorly Zoo & Aquarium

In 2012, travel website TripAdvisor named Omaha's Henry Doorly Zoo & Aquarium the nation's top zoo. The attraction has come a long way from its beginnings as Riverside Park, a city park founded in 1894. The park's menagerie grew, and the Omaha Zoological Society was organized in 1952 to help improve conditions for the animal collection. In 1963, Margaret Hitchcock Doorly donated $750,000 to the zoo with the stipulation that the zoo be named for her late husband, Henry Doorly, publisher of The World-Herald. The zoological society in 1965 was reorganized to run the zoo as a nonprofit organization.

Dennis Pate
Zoo Director and CEO

The Cat Complex, one of the largest in North America, opened in 1977, specifically as a breeding facility for endangered big cats. The zoo continued to grow in the 1980s and 1990s, adding such attractions as Mutual of Omaha's Wild Kingdom Pavilion, Lied Jungle (the world's largest indoor rain forest when it opened), Scott Aquarium and the Lozier IMAX Theater. Most of this growth was overseen by Dr. Lee "Doc" Simmons, its widely respected director. Other exhibits have followed, including the Desert Dome (the world's largest indoor desert), Kingdoms of the Night and Expedition Madagascar.

Now the zoo is preparing for more changes. Current Director and CEO Dennis Pate has envisioned a master plan that calls for a total redesign of the zoo over the next 10 to 15 years. While some of the newer exhibits will remain, many of the animals will be relocated within the zoo, and new animals will be added. Instead of species exhibits such as the Cat Complex, the zoo will be divided into the regions of the world from which its animals come. For example, the lions will join the African section that also will be home to giraffes, cheetahs, hoofstock, rhinos, wild dogs and elephants.

Changes already have started. Scott Aquarium was remodeled and reopened in 2012. An education center was added. The old Rosenblatt Stadium area was turned into more parking with an Infield at the Zoo memorial to commemorate the stadium. A new entrance and remodeled gift shop and visitor services area have opened.

But the most important parts of the zoo are the animals and the education about conservation of our natural treasures. The zoo is an accredited member of the Association of Zoos and Aquariums and participates in its species survival plans.

The five lion cubs have been immensely popular since their births. Anyone listening to young visitors at the exhibit will realize how captivated they are by Zuri, Taj, Kya, Leela and Josiri. Children rattle off facts and tell stories about the lions. While the cubs eventually will move on to other zoos, they always will be loved in Omaha.

Zoo staff

Zoo trainers, from left:
Mike Verbrigghe
Jenna Kocourek
Corissa Bartel
Hilary Merkwan
Ryan Whisney
Alan Holst
Agnieszka Podraza
Not pictured: Brandi Keim

Omaha World-Herald staff

Carol Bicak
author

Chris Machian
photographer

Kent Sievers
photographer

Omaha World-Herald Co. 1314 Douglas St. Omaha, NE 68102-1811
Second Edition ISBN: 978-0-615-87516-3
Printed by Walsworth Publishing Co. Marceline, MO

Book Editor
Dan Sullivan

Designer
Christine Zueck-Watkins

Photo Imaging
Jolene McHugh

Editors
Pam Richter, Pam Thomas, Dan Golden, Dana Carlson, Bob Glissmann

Intellectual Property Manager
Michelle Gullett

Print and Production Coordinators
Pat "Murphy" Benoit and Wayne Harty

Director of Marketing
Rich Warren

President and Publisher
Terry Kroeger

Executive Editor
Mike Reilly